Bedtime Rhymes

Compiled by John Foster

Illustrated by Carol Thompson

Oxford University Press

Oxford   New York   Toronto

Oxford University Press, Great Clarendon Street, Oxford OX2 6DP

Oxford   New York
Athens Auckland Bangkok Bogota Bombay
Buenos Aires Calcutta Cape Town Dar es Salaam
Delhi Florence Hong Kong Istanbul Karachi
Kuala Lumpur Madras Madrid Melbourne
Mexico City Nairobi Paris Singapore
Taipei Tokyo Toronto Warsaw

and associated companies in
Berlin Ibadan

Oxford is a trade mark of Oxford University Press

This selection and arrangement © John Foster 1998
Illustrations © Carol Thompson 1998
First published 1998

John Foster and Carol Thompson have asserted their moral
right to be identified as the authors of this work.

A CIP catalogue record for this book is available
from the British Library

ISBN 0 19 276166 8 (paperback)
ISBN 0 19 276205 2 (hardback)

Printed in Belgium

Contents

Bedtime, Bedtime — Tony Mitton — 8

Bedtime, Please! — Judith Nicholls — 9

Before the Bath — Corinna Marsh — 10

The Slippery Soap Song — John Foster — 11

Hair-Washing Night — Jack Ousbey — 12

Time For Bed — Patricia Leighton — 14

Books at Bedtime — Wes Magee — 16

Bed's Best — Kaye Umansky — 18

Who's in Bed? — Wes Magee — 20

The Bedtime Cuddle Rhyme — Mike Jubb — 21

Goodnight — Julie Holder — 22

Fee, Fi, Fo, Fum — Tony Bradman — 23

My Crocodile — Tony Mitton — 24

Dreams — Tony Mitton — 25

In the Middle of the Night — John Foster — 26

Magical Song — Jack Ousbey — 28

Bedtime, Bedtime

Bedtime, bedtime,
that's-what-Daddy-said-time.

Bedtime, bedtime,
stories-to-be-read-time.

Bedtime, bedtime,
cuddle-up-with-Ted-time.

Bedtime, bedtime,
rest-my-sleepy-head-time.

Bedtime, bedtime,
sssssssssshhhhhhhh . . .

Tony Mitton

Bedtime, Please!

One, two,
off with that shoe!
Three, four,
socks on the floor!
Five, six,
no more tricks!
Seven, eight,
you are LATE!
Nine, ten,
I won't tell you again!

Judith Nicholls

Before the Bath

It's cold, cold, cold
And the water shines wet,
And the longer I wait
The colder I get.

I can't quite make
Myself hop in
All shivery-cold
In just my skin.

Yet the water's warm
In the tub, I know
So—one, two, three,
And IN I go!

Corinna Marsh

The Slippery Soap Song

It slips through your fingers.
It slides, slides, slides
Under the water where
It hides, hides, hides.

Slippery soap,
Slippery soap,
You haven't a hope
Of catching the soap.

It slips through your hands.
It glides, glides, glides
Down towards the taps where
It hides, hides, hides.

Slippery soap,
Slippery soap,
You haven't a hope
Of catching the soap.

John Foster

Hair-Washing Night

Here comes Jason,
Here comes John;
Here comes Joey
With his rain-hat on.

John's big towel
Is fluffy and blue,
Jason has a bottle
Of yellow shampoo.

John has a brush,
Jason has a comb
And very special soap
In the shape of a gnome.

Under goes Jason,
Under goes John;
Under goes Joey
With his rain-hat on.

Scrub-a-rub one head,
Rub-a-dub two;
Soap suds flying—
Yellow shampoo.

'Jason,' says John,
'Just look at that.
Joey's hair's still
Under his hat.'

Out goes Jason,
Out goes John;
Out goes Joey
With his rain-hat on.

Jack Ousbey

13

Time For Bed

No more telly,
time to go to bed.

Climb the stairs slowly,
tread by tread.

Go to the bathroom,
clean your teeth.

Before you climb into bed
look underneath!

Jump in bed with teddy,   hold him tight.

Say 'goodnight' three times for luck

and switch
     off
       the light.

Patricia Leighton

15

Books at Bedtime

Here a wizard casts a spell.
Here big giants roar and yell.

Here are rabbits having fun.
Here's an island in the sun.

Here the tortoise wins the race.
Here's a rocket lost in space.

Here are children on a beach.

Here's a magic, flying peach.

Here green monsters come and go.
Here's old Santa in the snow.

Here's the wolf at Gran's front door.
Eleven books piled on the floor . . .

Wes Magee

Bed's Best

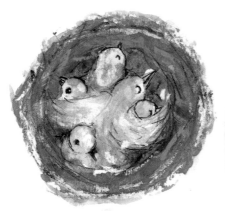
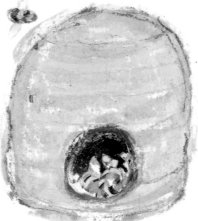

A nest is best for a bird,
A hive is best for a bee,
Moles and voles
Are best in holes

But bed's the best
for me.

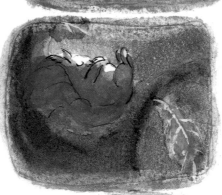

A cat can nap on a mat,
A squirrel can curl in a tree,
Fish have dreams
In ponds and streams

But bed's the best
for me.

A sheep can sleep in a field,
A cow is best in a shed,

But teddy and me,
We both agree,

We like it best in bed.
PHIL

Kaye Umansky

Who's in Bed?

Who's tucked-up
   with me in bed?
Peter Panda,
   One-eared Ted,
Steady Freddy,
   Wizard Mac,
Floppy Dog
   and Jumping Jack.
Silly Snake
   and Pirate Smee
all tucked-up
   in bed with me!

Wes Magee

The Bedtime Cuddle Rhyme

Cuddle me, cuddle me, cuddle me tight,
Kiss me when you say, 'Goodnight';
Then just as you turn out the light,
Cuddle me, cuddle me, cuddle me tight.

Mike Jubb

Goodnight

Goodnight goodnight
Sleepy head
Throw back the covers
And roll into bed.
Wink at the stars
Wave at the moon
Close your eyes now
You'll be fast asleep soon.

Julie Holder

22

Fee, Fi, Fo, Fum

Fee, fi, fo, fum,
Look out in there—
Here I come!

If you're awake
And not asleep,
Under the bedclothes
I will creep.

If you're awake
And not asleep,
I'll tickle your toes
Till I make you squeak!

Fee, fi, fo, fum,
Look out in there—
Here I come!

Tony Bradman

23

My Crocodile

My crocodile is very small.
He has no claws or teeth at all.
He doesn't scratch.
He doesn't bite.
He's safe to take to bed at night.

For when he's there, I'm glad to say,
He helps to snap bad dreams away.

Tony Mitton

Dreams

I dreamed of a dragon
with big, sharp claws.
I dreamed of a giant
with great, loud roars.
I dreamed of a monster
who asked me to play.
Then when I woke up
they all went away.

Tony Mitton

In the Middle of the Night

In the middle of the night
When you are sleeping,
Who comes creeping?
Who comes peeping?

Mouse comes creeping.
Mouse comes peeping.

Cat comes creeping.
Cat comes peeping.

In the middle of the night
When you are sleeping.
Who comes creeping?
Who comes peeping?

Mum comes creeping.
Mum comes peeping.
Shoos away the mouse.
Shoos away the cat.
Tucks you in
And leaves you
Soundly
            soundly
                        soundly
Sleeping.

John Foster

Magical Song

If you listen at night
When you put out the light,
And the moonshine comes into your room;
At the end of the day
You may hear, faraway,
A magical, musical tune.

And the tune someone's playing
Will seem to be saying,
It's time to be counting out sheep;
This magical song
Doesn't last very long,
It ends as you're falling asleep.

Jack Ousbey

We are grateful to the following for permission to publish their poems for the first time in this collection:

John Foster: 'In the Middle of the Night' and 'The Slippery Soap Song', both Copyright © John Foster 1998. **Julie Holder:** 'Goodnight', Copyright © Julie Holder 1998. **Mike Jubb:** 'The Bedtime Cuddle Rhyme', Copyright © Mike Jubb 1998. **Patricia Leighton:** 'Time For Bed', Copyright © Patricia Leighton 1998. **Wes Magee:** 'Books at Bedtime' and 'Who's in Bed?', both Copyright © Wes Magee 1998. **Tony Mitton:** 'Bedtime, Bedtime', 'My Crocodile', and 'Dreams', all Copyright © Tony Mitton 1998. **Judith Nicholls:** 'Bedtime, Please', Copyright © Judith Nicholls 1998. **Kaye Umansky:** 'Bed's Best', Copyright © Kaye Umansky 1998, reprinted by permission of the author c/o Caroline Sheldon Literary Agency.

We also acknowledge permission to include previously published poems:

Tony Bradman: 'Fee, Fi, Fo, Fum', first published by Heinemann in *A Kiss on the Nose*, Copyright © 1985 Tony Bradman, reprinted by permission of The Agency (London) Ltd. All rights reserved and enquiries to The Agency, 24 Pottery Lane, London W11 4LZ. **Jack Ousbey:** 'Magical Song', first published in *Tots TV* magazine (Fleetway, 1994), and 'Hair Washing Night', first published in a slightly different form in *Poems from the Sac Magique* by Jack Ousbey (Scholastic, 1994), both Copyright © Jack Ousbey 1994, reprinted here by permission of the author.